FUEL HOW INFLUENCES PUBLIC TRANSPORT NEED

JOHN LOK

Copyright © John Lok
All Rights Reserved.

This book has been published with all efforts taken to make the material error-free after the consent of the author. However, the author and the publisher do not assume and hereby disclaim any liability to any party for any loss, damage, or disruption caused by errors or omissions, whether such errors or omissions result from negligence, accident, or any other cause.

While every effort has been made to avoid any mistake or omission, this publication is being sold on the condition and understanding that neither the author nor the publishers or printers would be liable in any manner to any person by reason of any mistake or omission in this publication or for any action taken or omitted to be taken or advice rendered or accepted on the basis of this work. For any defect in printing or binding the publishers will be liable only to replace the defective copy by another copy of this work then available.

Print Published

All rights reserved. This book or any portion thereof may not be reproduced or used in any manner whatsoever without the express written permission of the publisher except for the use of brief quotations in a book review or scholarly journal.

Contents

Preface

This book research question :Has it relationship between airline fuel price rising or falling and the vehicle fuel consumers? How fuel price can influence public transport need to passengers? What factors can influence public transport to passengers needs?

This book aims to let economic students who can learn how to use behavioral economic method to predict why the airline fuel price will rise or fall can influence public transport passengers need. I hope any airline company management leader who can learn how to apply behavioral economic method to predict when fuel price rising in order to reduce fuel cost to airlines. In my books, I shall indicate what airline industry itself factors cause the fuel price will raise as well as what the other industries' external threat factors can cause fuel cost rising to airline industry.

Prologue

CHAPTER I

Fuel price rising or decreasing factor

1.1 Positive social change influence to vehicle fuel consumers

What suitation is positive social change to vehicle fuel consumers. We are entering globalizational competitive society, such as airline fuel case, if the country, e.g. US is increasing vehicle consumers in this year, then US vehicle fuel demand will increase. So, the US vehicle fuel price will be caused to increase. Due to much vehicle fuel demand increases in US this year, so foreign fuel import and US fuel manufacturers will increase to supply to US for vehicle market in this year, due to many US vehicle consumers need to buy fuel to drive their vehicles in US. However, due to fuel natural resource will have limited number to be supplied to manufacture airline fuel, due to much fuel is used to manufacture vehicle fuel in US this year. So, it will cause airline fuel manufacturing and supply shortage challenge. Due to this year, US decreases airline fuel supply, but the US airlines demands fuel number is still increasing. Consequently, vehicle fuel increasing demand factor will cause airline fuel price to be rised in US this year.

For example, air tickets can be bought from internet, so travellers won't need to go to travel agent to buy conventienty. It is due to the global travel industry is increasingly competition. Thus, global travel industry competition will bring negative social change to influences fuel price rising because it will increase traveller numbers and airline flight times to fly. When, traveller's travelling desire demand numbers will be grown up fastly, then their online electronic-ticket buying or consumption behaviors will be rise. Thus, it will also cause online e-ticket price is decreased to attract many travellers to choose to buy e-ticket from online channel more than paper-ticket visiting travel agent channel. Thus, it is negative social change influences to cause fuel price rising due to plane flight flying times will increase and airline company will increase demand to buy many fuel to prepare to fly often. When fuel demand will rise, then the fuel sellers will rise fuel price in possible. Thus, airline industry global competition will being negative social change to influence fuel price raising up and air ticket price falling down to attract many traveller numbers to choose to buy among different travel agents.

Negative social change influence

What suitation is positive social change. I shall indicate economic growth example. When one country has better economic development in the year. Then, employers will have more effort to do businesses. Then, they will create many jobs to provide to the country citizen to do. When, these unemployed people have jobs to do, they will have extra income to save. They can spend extra to prepare to spend to enjoy their entertainment every year, such as travelling. Thus, the positive social change will influence traveller number increasing, then the plane fliging flying times will also increase, it will cause planes need to use much fuel to fly. The result, it will also increase fuel demand, but the fuel natural resource number will decrease , so fuel supply will also decrease. Finally, it will also cause fuel price to be risen.

Also, I shall indicate the financial risk of airline industry evidence from Cathay Pacific airways and China airlines against key determinants of which include interest rate, exchange rate and fuel price risk for the period of January 1996 year to December 2011 year. During this period, these key external factors which were the most serious influence to cause these two airlines choose to change their strategic behaviors.

Due to any these financial risks is difficult to predict and it was also changing often, these factors will also affect any airlines stock returns which arise from changing economic conditions, e.g. fuel price movements and fluctuations in exchange rates. These external unpredicted changing factors will attribute to the air tickets cyclical demand, capital investment, fixed costs of labor and landing rights to this global airline industry.

However, the relationship between fuel price and stock prices varies across economies. The effects of oil price changes in sub-sector indices, such as wood, paper and printing, insurance and electricity. In the past, on global stock exchange market was positively significant in 2011 year. Otherwise, with respect to the U.S.A. aviation industry, some economists suggested that global airlines stock returns were negatively to percentage change in fuel prices related to any airline firm value, e.g. Qantas and Air New Zealand were negatively share price growth to fuel price risk in the short term in the 2011 year.

Thus, it brings this question. Whether positive or negative social change will be one important factor to impact fuel price rising. I feel positive social or negative social change will be one important factor to impact fuel price rising. The reason is such as below:

Nowadays, airline transportation demands are increasing, due to many travelers need to catch planes to travel as well as many cargoes need to be carried to planes to transport to different countries to sell. It seems aviation transportation industry is important to influence the health of the global economy growth nowadays. However, ignorance of internal or external market dynamics, catching travelers business can be detrimental to airline profitability more than carrying cargoes business. Because the demands of travelling different countries' travelers' consumption are still more than the demands of businessmen carrying cargoes in any countries every year. Thus, the travel industry will increase demand to human travelling business more than cargo transportation business. However, the cargo flying transporation demand will rise, due to many global fast speed post businesses are growing. Base on both global cargo flying transportation demand and travellers' flying travelling demand are increasing. Thus, the fuel demand will increase, but the fuel supply will be shortage. So, it will cause fuel price rising consequently.

How can positive or negative social change influence any airlines' air ticket prices to be risen or fallen? In fact, the increase in petroleum price can have chance to affect airlines in a negative manner because increased oil prices have resulted in the reduction of services operations, the number of airline schedules flights, even airline bankruptcies.

Thus, it seems that plan travellers and air flying cargo transportation both demand have been increasing. This social increasing demand change factor, it will be the most influential cause the bad effects to cause airline industry share price reducing or reducing air ticket price or decreasing traveler numbers more than the other factors influence, such as inflation, terrorism, oil shortage, bank interest rate etc. unpredictable external suitation factors.

To support this hypotheses, this are my research questions, such as : Does a combination of terrorism and price of petroleum significantly influence airline profit changing mostly? The alternative hypothesis was base on a significant relationship exists between terrorism, price of petroleum and airline profitability more than other factors, such as inflation, bank interest rate or air ticket price changing of these factors influence. I shall indicate that the first assumption was that terrorism has a negative effect on airline profitability and another assumption was that only external factors as oil prices or terrorism affect airline profitability.

Terrorisms attack influence

Whether terrorisms attack will influence fuel price rises up or falls down. I feel terrorisms attack to any country, which will cause plan fuel price falls down. Because travellers will feel dangerous and worry about their life safety when they catch the plan to enter the country if the country has serious terrorisms attack risk to cause plan crash accidently.

However the effects of oil price and terrorism on airline profitability was limited to a regional perspective, e.g. the terrorism attack of plane crash event to USA on 11 Sept. After the terrorism attack happened on USA 11 Sept. incident of terrorism attack was restricted to events of skyjacking, attacks on oil production, refinery and distribution. Thus, USA on 11 Sept. terrorism attack will cause oil price falls down , due to it will influence travellers fear death , so who will reduce times to travel to USA after 11 Sept. date terrorism attack occurrence at the year. The oil sellers will reduce oil sale price to attract many airline companies to buy more supply, due to airlines will decrease demand to buy fuel to provide planes to fly when the traveller numbers has decreasing and flying times will be decrease also. Thus, the fuel price will be decreased consequently after the terrorism attacks to any country.

Other types of terrorist activities, such as attacks on financial targets or senior government officials could have an adverse effect on the petroleum and airline industry. I think the disruption of the production or distribution of petroleum because of incidents of terrorism was costly in terms of loss of business and the inflationary effect on fuel dependent products or services.

In fact, some airlines have adopted more fuel saving technology, so whose fuel consumption would not use more than other non fuel saving technology airlines. So, the owned fuel saving technology airlines which will buy less fuel to use. It means that they won't need fear fuel rising to increase their expenditure because they only need to buy less fuel to use and their fuel demand won't fall , even fuel price has risen.

However, it seems fuel price increasing will not be the only factor to influence the airline industry's traveler numbers decreasing, due it is possible that the airlines need to rise air ticket price to riase their profit, sue to their fuel cost has risen. However, due to some airlines which have fuel saving technology, so which can avoid to use more fuel to provide planes to use and which fuel costs will be reduced, then which can provide cheaper air ticket fare prices to compare the non fuel saving technology airlines. The result will cause some non owned fuel save technological airlines will lose travelling customers in this global airline travelling market, also the non fuel saving technology airlines need to renew their fuel technology if which want to keep their competitive abilities to avoid to close down their businesses.

Can airline fuel self-organization avoid
fuel price rising cost

I feel one airline fuel self-organization can avoid fuel price rising to influence cost rising because it doesn't often buy any fuel from fuel suppliers. However, there are some airlines which are the characteristic of airline fuel self organization and they are present in that both of oil fuel production and providing flights service in airline industry. So, these airline fuel self organizations can control the oil fuel price by themselves. However, one airline fuel self organization is also evident in efforts by businesses acts of terrorism against economic targets by adopting proactive steps, such as airline and airport security. So, it seems airline fuel self organization can reduce the risk to avoid oil price raising and terrorism attacks to raise cost in airline industry risk management sector.

Beside, these airline fuel self organizations which have high technology of fuel efficient aircrafts, the use of one aircraft model, the adoption of direct routes versus customer loyalty programs and other operational cost reductions are strategies for increased profitability. It seems these airline fuel self organizations can solve oil price, terrorism etc. external factor influences to raise cost.

Instead of high technology of fuel efficient aircrafts and airline fuel self organization methods can solve terrorism attacks and oil price rising risks. However, I believe that there are other risks are caused to these airline fuel self organizations to raise their airline cost possibly. The risks include such as user factor, such as culture, tradition, education ; economic factor, such as costs, human resources and macro economic factor, such as political stability, economic development, educational policy, health policy, environmental policy. However, these risks occurrences are resulting in the relationship of cause and effect events. These events are not directly observable. Such as, the complexity of relationship between terrorism and airline profitability. Hence, if global airline industry can predict when those risks occur to do protective strategic behavior. It is possible that which can understand when these risk events will occur and to adopt their protective strategic behaviors to influence their outcomes to be positive to avoid any external risk threats on the long term. However, I think hierarchy, airlines fuel self organization efficiency methods which are as possible predictors of user preferences to avoid risk threat events to cause whose airline businesses cost rising to cause failure occurrences in airline industry.

Can tourism industry influence airline profitability

In my study, I suppose terrorism and the price of petroleum both factors which had properties of distinct and interrelated close relationship to raise airline cost. Moreover, these variables (terrorism and the price of petroleum) displayed differentiation, self replication, efficiency and hierarchy which can cause risk events to airline industry. However, I also think the other internal and external threat factors of airline industry, such as inflation, bank interest rate, business model, service quality, airline fuel or plane engine technology, air ticket pricing, brand loyalty, airline strategic management, government policy and fuel hedging of these factors which can also raise the risks to threaten any airlines existence in airline industry.

There are two basic business models in tourism industry. They are network (full service) and low cost (discount) carriers. The network carrier model employs diversification strategy by increased domestic destinations, serving international routes, providing diverse seating arrangements (business, economy and first class), maintaining a complex system of offering high quality service. Otherwise, low cost (discount) airlines focus on lower air fares. To keep operating costs down, discount airlines offer shorter routes and provide point-to-point destinations rather than through sophisticated flights are primarily in domestic destinations. So, discount airlines operate a common model aircraft fleet, offer a single seating arrangement and cheaper flight services offered to compare network airlines. However, these two basic business models have their unique competitive abilities to provide any airlines existence in tourism industry nowadays.

In fact, natural resource of oil is decreasing in our earth. But as the same time, human demand is increasing and oil supply is decreasing, so it also causes the oil fuel price is increasing to supply to airline industry. It influences not only to airline industry, it also impacts of higher oil fuel price to tourism, such as expansion of airports are made based on expected demand increase.

Tourism has been proven to many adverse events, including terrorism, flight disruptions. Beside, the bad natural climate change influences, such as the volcanic ash cloud event occurred in April 2010 year. So, airline industry need to concern climate change because it will cause high fuel prices indirectly. For example, the event occurred the extreme increase in operating costs for airlines in 2008 year, due to unprecedented prices for aviation fuel also meant, that despite the introduction of fuel charges, so this event causes the global tourism industry recorded losses seriously. Even if alternative fuels become commercially available for airlines which are still likely to be more expensive than present aviation fuel.

Higher airfares in the future are likely to lead to reduction in travel and cause tourists to shift from more distant to closer destination. When some of the economic responses to higher oil prices are obvious assessing the overall economic impacts on tourism is difficult. However, long term changes in global oil price rises will be similar to global changes in other commodity prices, exchange rates and income. It is therefore important to consider the impact of high oil prices on tourism from a general equilibrium perspective rather than relying only on bottom partial equilibrium approaches.

However, I believe tourism and airline industries have close relationship, such as tourism and airline industries are likely to suffer in an environment of high oil prices. Given that tourism destinations receive tourists from a range of origins, it would be useful to understand of some countries are increasing oil prices than others. Such as the net oil importing countries are selling higher oil prices than oil exporting countries generally. For example, New Zealand is an oil import country to provide planes for international visitor arrivals, so its oil fuel price is usually higher to charge to NZ airlines because any NZ airlines need to pay to foreign countries to buy any oil more expensive price. So, NZ airlines usually charge higher airfares to its visitors to compare the other exporting oil countries' airlines. It will impact NZ has negative influence to domestic tourism industry as well as planes need will also be decreased , due to NZ charge high fuel price to cause air ticket price to be raised.

In economic theory, on income effects indicate negative

impacts on tourism demand, the exact effects of higher oil fuel prices for specific destinations are far from clear. However, airline industry's different market segments show different sensitivities to air ticket fares changes.

On the first hand, if the visitors are long destinations generally wealthier than average and therefore potentially less affected, as energy costs would be a smaller proportion of their income compared will be those from less wealthy groups. Thus, the more wealthier travelers who won't decrease travelling desire, even the fuel price raises to case the air ticket price to be increased.

On the second hand, oil prices don't translate into higher transport costs especially not on air routes that are highly competitive and that are maintained for strategic reasons. So, non air transportation industry won't influence customer number to be decreased easily.

On the third hand, many other factors shape tourists' decision making, including emotion drivers or those related to images, fashions and perceptions. Increasing environmental protection awareness of tourists could also be an important factor to influence tourism consumption, instead of oil fuel price raising causes air ticket fares raising factor to reduce traveler numbers. However, oil price raising reason causes also due to high use of cars, vans and domestic air transport in some countries, e.g. Hong Kong, China countries, there are many people like to buy cars to drive. So, the private driver numbers are increasing demand to cause these countries' oil fuel prices raise in the short time suddenly. It implies airlines need to consider their country car number whether is increasing or decreasing. If their country car number is increasing, it is possible to cause fuel price to be risen up because car demand is increasing to need to use more fuel and it has less supply of fuel in the year. Otherwise, if their country car number is decreasing, it is possible to cause fuel price to be fallen down because car demand is decreasing to need to use less fuel and it has more supply of fuel in the year.

Is fuel price rising only factor to cause airline risk
in short term

In long run, fuel raising price will not cause risk to airline, due to implications of changes to supply and demand side conditions of oil fuel energy may differ qualitatively. For example, due to investment responses of producers, consumers and governments in alternative energy sources and more energy efficient plants, vehicles are supplied in order to achieve oil fuel price can't be risen seriously.

However, I believe oil fuel rising charge will be an important factor to influence global airline ticket fares to be increased in the short term to cause risk because oil fuel rising charge will be influenced to raise any airlines pressure from other unpredicted factor risk influences.

Firstly, on the bank interest changing factor, e.g. bank interest rate rising which only attract more bank saving. But it can not influence the bank savers who choose to reduce relax time to go to other countries travelling. Otherwise, when the bank savers can save more money to earn higher interest in banks, who will prefer to choose to use their saving to consume travelling. Due to who can earn higher interest rate after a period of saving time. So, I believe who behavioral travelling consumption will be raised when the banks will raise interest rate, then the bank savers won't choose to save more money in banks. So it is possible that who will withdraw more money to consume to go to travelling from banks. It seems bank interest rate changing won't influence bank savers' behavioral travelling consumption to be reduced.

Secondly, on the exchange rate changing factor, although any country's exchange changing will cause other countries' money value to be fallen down or risen up. However, it won't influence any travelers' behavioral consumption to be reduced seriously. Although, it is possible that the traveler won't spend too much to go to shopping when who travel to the another country and arrive the country. But, it is not possible to influence the traveler decides to reduce consumption to buy any air ticket to go to travelling in short time.

Thirdly, any country inflation also can not reduce travelers' travelling consumption easily because inflation can influence consumers who choose to buy cheaper foods and clothing and reduce entertainments in their every day life. But, one country's inflation can not influence it's citizen do not spend much travelling expenditure because travelers only spend one time or two times of travelling every year usually. So, the travelling expenditure rate of any households is not too much to compare daily essential expenditure.

So, it seems that bank interest rate and exchange rate changing and inflation won't influence any travelers' travelling consumption of decisions to be reduced easily in short time. Otherwise, if the oil fuel price raises too much, then global airlines' cost will be raised in long term. So, the airlines only choose to increase their air fare prices to aim to avoid loss possibly in long term. It seems that oil fuel raising price and bank interest rate and exchange rate changing and inflation factors will have direct influence airline income in long term.

Methods to solve rising air fare

prices to decrease travellers'demand

Biofuels energy increases supply

I suggest these methods how to avoid the oil raising price factor to cause airline air fare prices to be risen to lead the risk of traveler numbers to be reduced as below:

The first method: Whether aviation fuel markets will have what benefits from biofuels supply to planes. I shall refer the scope includes trends in jet fuel price, airline response to fuel price, increases and volatility and environmental goals for aviation. The aviation fuel supply industry includes production, distribution and consumption of aviation fuel and it outlines players in the aviation fuel supply chain. For example, at each airport, fuel supply chain organization and fuel sourcing could differ with regard to the role of oil companies, airlines, airport owners and operators and airport service companies. However, major jet fuel purchasers are airlines, general aviation operators, corporate aviation and the military, with most of the jet fuel in global different countries demanders being used for domestic commercial and civilian flights carrying passengers, cargos or both.

Commercial aviation fuel efficiency has improved dramatically over time, largely due to aircraft and engine upgrades and operational and air traffic control improvements. So, it seems that fuel supply factor can influence airline fare prices majorly. However, jet fuel prices generally correlate with prices of crude oil and other refined petroleum products, such as diesel. So, increasing prices and the persistent price volatility of jet fuel markets import airline industry finances in any countries.

However, airlines use various strategies to manage aviation fuel price certainty, including financial hedges, increased vertical integration and adjustments in aircraft utilization and size to avoid the jet fuel raising price risk.

Investments in alternative aviation fuel could be a mechanism to diversity expose to the price of petroleum. It seems the use of alternative aviation fuel would serve to diversify the fuel mix to reduce the risk of jet fuel monopoly raising price threat. If a diversified fuel mix were to avoid either fuel raising price in short term or to avoid fuel raising price in long term. Potential benefits include reduced actual fuel costs from only choice of jet fuel supply increased price certainty and lessened fuel costs. This diversify could allow airlines to become more consistently profitable and to make other investments in their businesses.

So, biofuels have potential to meet aviation industry needs, possibly including managing risks of upward fuel price trends and fuel price volatility and avoid risks with greenhouse gas emissions. So, the aviation fuels market could use biofuels to reduce greenhouse gas emission and mitigate long-term upward price trends, fuel price volatility or both.

What are the challenges of high priced oil for aviation? In fact, nowadays not the resources of oil as such, but much more the insecurity of supply, due to geopolitical instability in combination with a tight oil market makes a scenario with much higher oil prices than the world is currently experiencing not unlikely.

Aviation is completely dependent upon oil as its fuel source. Since no practical energy substitute is readily available for commercial aviation, a scarcity of petroleum relative to demand will present a major aviation policy. In addition, efficiency gains, due to operational measures and new aircraft medium term. In particular, it has been demonstrated that the annual reduction rate in fuel consumption traffic unit is not a constant, but is itself also falling, in contrast to past estimates.

So, a high-priced oil scenario will have severe consequences for demand, airline revenues, the competitive position of airports and eventually airline networks, strategies and fleet development. In particular, transfer demand, short-haul and leisure traffic can be expected to be heavily affected by high oil prices, due to their relative high price sensitivity. Also, different countries' governments or/and airlines are valuable to research another new and potential biofuel energy to substitute oil energy to supply our planes to reduce the threat of oil monopoly supply to influence the cause of air fare raising prices. Because the elasticity is very high to travelers, when the travelers feel air fares are rising high or even low level to influence travelers who will choose not to buy the air tickets to go to travel easily.

Whether will the fuel (oil based inputs) risk be high to compare other costs, e.g. engineering maintenance, employees salaries, general cleaning, security office expenses etc. expenditures to airlines? If the probability-weighted upside effect on firm value when a risk is resolved favorably is greater the risk than the probability-weighted downside effect if the risk is resolved badly, then expected value work not be enhanced by hedging. So, the risk will be resolved badly to any commercial airlines.

Airlines are an interesting case because the direct effect of source of risk resides squarely within the no offset in revenue functions (unlike for oil producers, for example), so value effects from costs feed directly into equity value. Most directly, the risk source is fuel costs to commercial airlines. Jet fuel is of course, a mix product of crude oil, so airlines indirectly face oil price risk. There are reasons to expect that airlines' fuel costs might to convex in oil price (i.e. absent any hedging). For example, oil prices, being generally pro-cyclical in recent times, tend to be highest when airline demand is strong.

In conclusion, airlines are therefore apt to use more high priced fuel than low-priced fuel over time. Airlines can raise air fare benefit is limited by the elasticity of demand. Also, cost functions could be influenced from fuel cost corresponds to upturns in economic activity overall (due to demand pressures on oil related prices), so it causes that airline's capacity delivers their services given their level of fixed capital. The essence of airlines basis risk in the case of jet fuel is essentially the time profile of the refining margin between crude and jet fuel, or the time profile of the price differential between other refined distillates and jet fuel. Thus, it is far from clear that risk management with oil is sure to add value to any airlines. It seems the impact of airline energy and any countries' domestic or foreign airline passenger travel numbers which have direct close relationship.

Reducing terrorism occurrence

Can reduce terrorism occurence to reduce airline failure risk? It needs to judge to determine if a combination of terrorism and the price of petroleum significantly predicted airline profitability and which variable whether the further period was the most significant between the terrorism occurrence and the price of petroleum influence.

I suggest that different countries' governments or airlines need to collect samples of financial records from which country's any airline commercial passengers and cargo airlines on costs of fuel and any airline profitability. Also, gathering the terrorism data were comparison of terrorist attacks on petroleum in oil-producing nations, and incidents of high jacking aboard any country's aircraft.

When any countries' airlines or governments can judge whether the impact of airline energy and terrorism risk level is high or middle or low level. Then, which can use this sample data to measure how to do positive social change to decide either ought rise or reduce employment in commercial aviation industry, or ought need to invest other higher commercial activity in tourist and other travel related service businesses and when is the most right time to adopt of green technologies by the civil aviation manufacturing industry after the terrorism attacks occurrence to any country. It seems that any countries' governments or airlines which ought concern that the event of when the terrorism attacks will occur and gather past sample data to predict when the next time terrorism attacks event will be occurred and the risk will be high or middle or low level to influence global airline industry development.

Will airline industry's ticket price elasticity be influenced by demand and supply factor
In fact, the airline industry is largely dependent on the supply of the oil industry. Otherwise, the oil industry is inelastic. However, the increase or decrease of the price of airfare is directly related to the increase or decrease of the oil's price to fuel the aircrafts because there has no any new energy which can be substituted to oil fuel to airline industry.

So, it seems oil fuel producers are monopolies to control its sale price to be raised easily. Another factor that can affect airline industry to be directly targeted by a tragedy brought about by terrorism. The past four years, from 2001 year to 2005 year, there had been at least $40 billion worth of losses in the airline industry because of the September 11 date terrorism attacks in 2000 year. There had been an expected and significant decrease in the demand for the airline industry services because of the attacks that involved planes hijacking and crashing into key locations like the World Trade Center and the Pentagon in USA. Although, terrorism attacks can bring risk to influence fuel price rising in airline industry. However, this risk occurrence to airline industry is only that after the terrorism attacks occurred. It is possible that terrorism attacks won't occur again in the future.

Otherwise, our concerning ought be the greenhouse emissions and how it affects global warming. The air quality would be better once this new regulations are adopted. However, it would affect large airlines. So, it would increase the price of airfares because of economic fees that airline companies have to cover. Air pollution can give a negative impact on the domestic or oversea owned airline companies for long term. If airlines' planes can use clean fuel to fly, e.g. biofuel, then it will bring benefits to global airlines for long term.

On the positive side, the environment would be healthier as the earth's temperature would rise, and greenhouse effect would be dramatically reduced. This positive effect can come at a cost that is greater than most people perceive. On the psychology view point on travelers, who will be more preferable to catch planes to go to different countries to travel, due to the chance of air pollution and global environmental warm issues will be reduced to low risk to influence our health if planes can use biofuel to be energy to fly in the future one day.

It seems that spending expenditure to research other non

polluted biofuel new energy is one solvable method to global airline industry in the future. To solve, any airlines or countries' governments or oil producers ought choose to spend more time to research new biofuel. Otherwise, the predicting when terrorism attacks event will be occurred, it is more difficult to predict the time more than researching to produce new biofuel energy method in the future. So, I recommend that researching the new biofuel energy or other kinds of energy to substitute the oil energy is the urgent behavioral economy which the airlines or oil producers or different countries' governments which need to concern nowadays.

CHAPTER II

Designing transportation system advantages

Nowadays, transportation and economic development have close relationship. Economic development stimulates transportation demand by increasing the numbers of workers commuting to and from work, customers traveling to and from services areas, and products being moving by lorries on the roads between products and customers. According to Bailey, Mokhtarian and Little (2008) indicated ''transportation route is past of distinct development pattern or road network and mostly described by regular street patterns as an important factor of human existence, development and civilization. The route network combined with increased road transportation investment result in changed levels of conveniently reflected through cost benefit analysis, savings in travel time, and other benefits. '' These benefits are noticeable in increased catchment areas for services and facilities , shops, schools, offices, banks and leisure activities.

What are the crisis of neglection to care transporation system ? Why do any countries need to design road transportation system? For example, the Japan country lacks design road trsnaportation system effectively. So, the crisis of road traffic fatalities will raise and the econominc influence will be changed. The crisis indicates more than 7,000 people die annually as a result of motor vehicle crashes in Japan. Driving when under the influence of alcohol is the leading cause of motor vehicle crash fatalities in both developed and developing countries. So, alcohol is the most serious factor to raise personal risk when drivers are driving in Japan. However, a number of studies have shown that deterring drink driving is an important way to cause fatalities. There is a demonstrative need for social change in Japan.

Japan has recently strengthened its already strict laws in order to reduce the number of alcohol related road fatalities. Those deforms lowered the legal blood alochol contant limit increased, the penalties for offenders. The Japan road traffic legal needs. Any driving a motor with a alcohol limit of 0.03 or higher Japan's maximum sentence is up to 3 years imprisonment or a fine not exceeding 500,000 yen dollars. Is law impact to reduce drinking alcohol to drive in Japan? What are economic influence of the crisis of road traffic fatalities in Japan?

The rational choice theory of offending suggests that offenders are active decision makers who influence a large number of variables into decision whether or not to commit an offence. On the cost-benefit analysis, it is the punishment a possible jail, large fines worth is the reward the convenience of driving home without the expause of a taxi and innovenience to the alcohol drivers in Japan. Instead of law reforms when it detects alcohol in the air exhaled from the alcohol and other offenders and it educates children about the dangers of drinking and it also explains why alcohol driving can also threaten drivers' life when who are drinking alcohol and driving behaviour in the same time in Japan.

On the economic influence hand, implementation of the policy deregulating alcohol sales and alcohol production did not appear to increase traffic fatalities among adult or teenage males or females in Japan. We found that male adult fatalities demonstrated a statistically significant decline following enactment of the deregulation policy in 1994 year. So, Japan implement law to threaten alcohol drinking behaviour is useful. It can influence the alcohol availability and consumption, alcohol production and sales, the 24 hours operated convenience stores or liquor discount stores incomes to be reduced. Even, Japan overall GDP is also reduced from the deduction of liquor alcohol production and sale, also the occurrence of traffic accident fatalities chances will be also reduced.

The Japanese economy has entered a rapid process of liberalization since the mid-1990 year. Many sectors previously under direct government control are now regulated by the competitive market place. The Japanese alcohol beverage market has changed. The entry of cheaper import alcohol products resulted in a encouragement of alcohol consumption to Japan drinking drivers and an raising of increasing of more import alcohol products supply to Japan. Although, it is beneficial to Japan GDP growth. But it also raise the occurrence of chance to traffic accidents rate to cause alcohol drinkers to be death or hurt when who choose drinking alcohol to drive at the same time in Japan. So, alcohol import can bring more consumption, but it can also raise many traffic accidents occurrence in Japan in the same time.

In conclusion, alcohol is not good for health to drink when the consumer often buys alcohol at drink habitually. So, if many Japanese, including the alcohol driving consumers and the alcohol non drinking consumers both who often buy different countries alcohol to drink daily. It will cause their bodies to be unhealth for long term in Japan. It is possible to increase Japan's government's medical expenses to assist the low income or poor people in the future. So, although alcohol import can raise Japan GDP growth in the short term, but it also raise Japan government's medical expenditure to the low income or poor Japanese long term in the future, So it's economic benefit will not good in the future if Japan still import much alcohol to sell in its country.

Many commercial users depend on road transport facilities, with movement of products and services from place to place on the roads, aspect of global and urban economic survival. Hence, developments of various transportation modes have become important to physical and economic developments. For example, urban locations with such relative advantages are found where different transport routes with high degree of connectivity, within the intra and inter urban road networks. On similarly, commercial activities like banking, retail/wholesale businesses and professional services can take advantage of nearness to concentration of activities attracted consumers service providers. This partly caused increase in demand for commercial space and its effects on commercial property values along commercial roads can be rose. However, some countries' roads need to provide pedestrian movements more than the businesses activities, e.g. shorten the time of lorries parking on the road to let pedestrian movements on the narrow road. If the country government did not consider the roads need to let more pedestrian movements or shorten the time of lorries parking on the road. It will cause traffic jam or traffic density of the individual roads. Hence, governments need to concern the locations of commercial property buildings and the relationship between the explanatory variables of the design road networks.

What are construction of roads design networks benefits? In fact, construction of roads increased substantially with the opening up of residential environments that also is getting much benefits from increasing demand for spaces in commercial properties. Many private companies, retail stores, commercial banks aggregate in the main roads of cities, which get advantage of opportunities afforded by locations near central of cities to attract many pedestrians concerning their businesses existence. This led to high concentration of vehicular and pedestrian movements. Specially along the access main roads in the central of cities. The main roads exhibits linkages to form networks of minor routes along which commercial properties locate. If commercial users are displaced residential users, causing sites to be at the highest and best uses with increases in the values of commercial properties. However, it seems road network development is affected by the compact nature of various routes that sometimes causes volume of traffic jam. Thus, demand for transport can't be treated solely as a derived demand road. Improved main and minor roads access an city or rural areas is a necessary (but not sufficient). Precondition for increased productivity, the UK Standing Advisory committee On Trunk Road Assessment (SACTRA, 1999) noted "various ways in which transport can affect economic growth, for example benefits include through reorganization and rationalization of production, distribution and land use: reducing labor costs by expanding catchment areas etc."

What is land use and road transport design system relationship? Land use refers to the whole range of human activity and of the built environment, and to some aspects of the natural environment. This is a way relationship between land use and road transport. Governments need to design how to use land and how to design road transportation systems. e.g. where are built the main roads and/or where are built the minor roads are the most suitable locations in the cities or rural areas ? If the main roads is located in the not suitable locations at the centers of the cities or rural, it will case the increasing traffic volumes and levels of congestion, including air pollution, noise, ground water pollution from run-off , loss of soil functions and loss of bio-diversity to natural environment. By influencing the spatial structure of locations in the urban environment, so land use planning can help to mitigate any negative effects resulting from land use changes.

Modelling and land use transportation interactions has become an important aspect of road design transport planning. On the one side, for example, design roads in urban centers, it can increase land use and it can also reduce employees or students catching buses or driving cars' time spending to go to workplaces or schools users. Hence, the land use and roads designing transportation can give benefits to residents and employment people to reduce time to wait buses or taxies etc. public transportations to go to workplaces or schools or shopping centers etc. anywhere. It seems to assist bus companies or taxi drivers to earn more income, On the other side, designing urban transport systems is also important . Increased densities mean more destinations become within convenient walking and cycling distances and consequently the use of these modes tends to be higher. Also in dese cities public transport systems are able to offer higher levels of service and operate more economically, when the provision of sufficient road space to meet potential demand becomes impractical. It aims to reduce the danger of driving or walking in urban areas. The transport modes (that is walking, cycling, public transport) and the extent of car dependence is less, due to driving users dependency is less on rural roads. Hence, building main roads can concentrate on designing convenience to pedestrian walking to close to their houses on the streets. However, poor transport design and land use can cause to spend too expenditure not only transport costs on governments and transport users both and also the costs of providing other services. These include the usual utilities and also education and health services as well as negative externalities , such as greenhouse gas emissions. Most such studies concluded that there are significant financial and economics cost advantage of inner city redevelopment compared with fringe development.

However, such policies won't necessarily be successfully, in particular because of the two ways road problem, they may result in additional private investments and employment opportunities flowing into the region, buy may equally result in population and employment opportunities flowing out of the target region because of the improved access to other centers. Hence governments need to analyze how to arrange the land use to assist the property developers to choose where are the suitable locations to build offices or factories or shopping centers or houses at capital or urban cities to adapt to whose the growth of living population. For example, to judge where the land use whether where main roads or junior roads are built where are the suitable locations to satisfy the lorry drivers to park their lorries are the safe locations ; to design the minor roads to let the pedestrians to feel no danger to walk on the streets when the cars are driven to near to the streets on the minor roads. Thus, the factor of choosing where the land use to design the main or minor roads areas, sizes and lengths and of the minor or major roads can influence the drivers and pedestrians feel safe or dangerous when who are driving whose cars on the roads or who are walking on the streets to arrive the offices, schools, cinemas, church, houses etc. destination.

Designing road transportation networks how to assist economic growth ? I feel it is not all transport investments will be equally effective in enhancing economic growth. Designing road transport investment is a necessary, but on its own not sufficient requirement to earn significant economic growth at either a national or regional level. There are conditions under three categories: economic conditions, investment conditions and political conditions. In fact, although in some circumstances, transport investment may be a necessary condition for enhancing economic growth, it is rarely on its own a sufficient condition. Other factors including the broader policy environment, need to be present if the investment is going to be successful in addressing regional economic objectives. My some suggestions the following key aspects as being most relevant including:

a. Scale economies for example, where these dominate, lower transportation costs through improved accessibility may encourage increased concentration of firms in core regions, until the point that diseconomies set in.

b. Size of the local market.

c. Local land and labor conditions.

d. The nature and scale of transport improvements.

e. The nature of backward and forward linkages
in the country 's local economy.

In any countries, road transportation improvements don't

guarantee increased economic development. To increase economic development, an improvement needs to assist any lorry drivers to drive in short trips to reduce transportation costs and shorten time driving on the road or to make transportation more reliable, e.g. reducing the numbers of traffic jams on any roads. A proper economic climate must also exist as well as other support services. With these factors to influence transportation improvements can become catalysts for economic expansion. However, road transportation improvement that intends to induce job creation, when employers need many lorry drivers to help them to transport products and to move products on the roads often. So, the employers need to employ many transportation workers and lorry drivers to help who to transport their products to send to clients, due to the transportation time is shorten and work efficiency is rasied, so the transportation times are also increasing every day when the road transportation roles are improved. On the other side, improving transportation can raise productivity when many customers need to buy many products and the lorry drivers may drive whose lorries to transport many products between factory and office or between factory to the client's home or between the shop and the client's on the road in the short time fast.

I recommend one model links in an overall road transportation network includes these four modes.

I. Maximizing use of the existing road highway system.

II. Extending or improving the multi-lane divides system local roads and connectors.

III. Continually improving the entire road highway network in response to business activities demand.

The improvement of modern road transportation successful factors include:

● How to improve the highway network

modernization includes obsolete interchanges and other segments of the road, transport network of new designs to improve the life and service of pedestrian walking streets, rebuilding certain in main or minor roads. To the extent that labor markets operate more efficiently and more jobs are created to raise economic expansion if our governments can improve road transportation system to design to satisfy business users demand when lorry drivers need to move or transport whose products on the streets, but who will not influence pedestrian are walking on the streets. Hence, excellent transportation design network can subsequent plan efforts, it can also rise economic efficiency, community and social effects, it can also encourage transportation users to attempt to drive lorries to transport products a lot of times in one day fast and who can also avoid traffic jams occurrence on the road easily. On the one side, economic development is a concept referring to the material aspects of community welfare. There are numerous factors need of development: growth in income and wealth, equitable distribution of income, decreased infant mortality rates, increased literacy rates. On the other side, economic growth means which is sustainable increase in community income and /or wealth. (wealth is the net of resources that generate income). It seems the link between transportation facilities and economic growth has close relationship. Good transportation facilities support economic growth by lowing the transportation costs of users of the transportation network, such as roads. Direct users benefits are reductions in travel, times and fuel consumption, increased reliability and increased safety in the movement of people and products, users' transportation costs are reduced, resources are used for other purpose.

The relationship between transport and economic development occur in two directions, in the sense that (i) land use and economic development are major drivers' of demand for transport (in terms of quantity , type, location and mode); and (ii) transportation investments and other initiatives (such as regulations, pricing) can influence levels, patterns and locations of economic development. The principal role of road transportation is to provide access between spatially separated locations for the business and household sectors, for both commodity (lands transportation) and person movements. For the business sector, this involves connections businesses and their input sources between business factories and other business shops and between business and their markets. For the households sector, it provides people with access to workplaces and education facilities, shops and social recreation, community and medical facilities etc. on the roads. I feel different countries' road transportation system can be self funded in the sense that the majority of the costs of transportation system investment operation and maintenance are either paid directly by users (for example, through car operating costs) are funded initially by governments and recovered from transport users (for example, through petrol duties and road user charges). Governments' road transportation system and their use also give rise to some external costs(externalities). These include global environmental impacts (greenhouse gas emissions) and local environmental and health impacts (for example, noise partial pollution and road accident costs). The direct effects of transportation investments are to reduce road transportation time and costs through reducing travel time, decreasing the operating costs of transportation and enhancing access to destinations within the road network. A good road transportation network also needs to reduce any economic disbenefits, for example where projects reduce congestion or the risk of injury. These incremental benefits of transportation investments may be measured through commercial cost benefit analysis. Other indirect consequences of road transportation network should also be considered when evaluating effects on productivity and the spatial pattern of economic development. Good road transportation design network benefits can include lower costs and enhanced accessibility, due to better transportation links and services expand markets for individual transportation using business and improved access to input.

The economic contribution of road transportation policy can be assessed from various perspectives. These include:
● Effects on aggregate economic welfare (e.g. the sum of consumer and which is the times of cost benefit analysis, as linking to transportation productivity effect.
● Micro economic, for example, enterprise or household level productivity effects.
● Macro economics, for example, contributions to GDP investment or employment and the spatial patterns of economic activity.
One key characteristics of road transportation is split between infrastructure and operations. Infrastructure refers to the right of way on which vehicles operate, which may include ancillary facilities to ensure efficient and effective operations (for example, traffic signals, railway stations). In developed countries, are in most transportation is operated by the private cars, road trucks, the majority of bus and coach services. In long term ,

overall purpose, to ensure transportation system helps to develop that maximizes the economic and social benefits and minimizes harm. Hence, governments need to concern who are their main target users to use every road. Such as the road is used to near to park and leisure, or local and national economic conditions, keep clean natural environment etc. facilities to provide different benefits to different target users to enjoy to use. It seems that good transportation networks designing can influence economic activities, shopping convenience or business convenience etc. activities to cause whether the country's economic behavior to achieve close relationship successfully. Possible relationship between road networks, location attribute, demand and supply and accessibility and commercial property values of these factors which will influence different countries' concerning to choose where to build main roads and sub minor roads in different cities and rural locations. However, I shall suppose hypotheses how governments to find the most suitable places to build main roads and sub minor roads to whose cities and rural. There is no significant relationship between commercial property values and individual contributions of explanatory variables to variability in commercial property values in whose countries.

In conclusion, I suggest methods how to design suitable transportation networks to governments to build, such as it is essential to establish a technique that may be useful for determining relative accessibility of locations in the network of main roads and sub minor roads. Even, when relative advantages are determined, there is need to develop models that will be useful for predicting commercial properly values. The model may become tool for professional estate surveyors and values to change their practice of using intuition to determine relative access of locations in a road network. Similarly, there is the need to predict the supply of, demand for, and fair market values of commercial properties by developers. Hence if the cities or rural locations can attract many businesses to build commercial properties, governments can build the main roads in the locations. Otherwise, if the cities or rural locations can not attract many businesses to build commercial properties, governments can build the sub minor roads in these locations. Hence, the main roads must have high transportation valuation to let big lorries to drive and park in these main roads easily and conveniently. It seems capital cities may not influence to build the main road factors. Natural environment, commercial properties values, the lands areas size and shape and pedestrian walking numbers on the streets and lorries available numbers on the areas will be other factors to influence where to build main roads in any cities or rural in the country.

In road concept, the route network consists of primary and secondary roads, known as main roads and minor roads respectively. Main roads are usually moderate or high capacity roads that are below highway level of service, carrying large volumes of traffic between areas in urban centers and designed for traffic between neighbors. They have intersections with collector and local streets and commercial areas, such as shopping centers, petrol stations and other businesses are located along such roads. In additions, main roads link up to expressways and freeways with inter-changes in cities or rural. Road network constitutes an important element in urban development , due to urban areas have many farms, gardens, forests , so roads and building needed to provide accessibility required by different land uses and the proper functioning of such urban areas depends an efficient transport network existence. In computing des, the network indicator are used to partition road network into different parts in reasonable way. The results in number of connection to describe density differences in road networks. The parameter records how many roads connect to each road in a network. For two roads with the same length, the ones in the dense area will connect to more roads than that in a sparse area and the connection differences will indicate the density differences to some extent, so road density can also be calculated as the total length of all known roads divided by the total land area in a road divided by the total land area in a road network. Hence, governments need to consider road length to decide how to build main or minor roads to design its transportation systems for businesses activities , such as driving lorries and parking lorries and products are been moving on the streets from roads easily and conveniently. As Wikipedia Contributors (2008) indicate that "transport networks are spatial structures designed to channel flows from the points of demand to points of supply and to link the points together in a transportation system. They are useful for transport network analysis to determine the flow of people, products, services and vehicles." Hence, governments need to research whether where the shopping centers, cinemas, houses, hospitals, schools, offices, factories etc. are located, then, which need to follow these location datas to predict the cars, lorries, taxies, buses etc. of the demand numbers of transportation users to design the lengths, width and distances and the construction of main and minor roads locations and their supply numbers in different capital cities or country roads. It aims to reduce traffic jams and shorten time and air pollution as well as increasing the available spaces to let the lorry drivers to move their logistc on the road easily and reducing the accidents occurrence when the pedestrians are walking on the streets. If the vehicles can be moved on the roads easily. It will also increase time efficiency and productivity to any businessmen. Hence, how to design of the main roads and/or minor roads in any capital or country cities. It will influence any country's economic growth long time in the future.

Underground train transportation needs to know passenger behaviour reasons

Understanding individual passenger behaviour is essential for the design MTR transportation, because who can choose to catch bus, taxi, tram, train ferry etc. different kinds of public transportation tools. Individual traveler who decides to catch which kinds of public transportation tools, it depends on whether the public transportation tool can provide real time travel information, liking link travel time schedule. So, MTR underground train needs to understand where it has terminal to give convenience to the local living areas of time travelers to choose to catch MTR easily. Although, MTR ticket fare is one factor to influence any passengers choice. But, those other factors can also influence them to choice. e.g. MTR any terminal location of convenience, short time travelling, none crowding in busy (peak) time, MTR platform waiting arrival time, none sudden MTR engineering machines broken accident events occurrence frequently etc. different factors, any one of these factors which can influence passengers who choose to catch MTR or other kinds of transportation tools.

Why route choice can influence passenger behavioural choice ? Usually, the busy time passengers will regard the route choice as a coordination problem to influence them to choose to catch which kinds of transportation tools. The route choice is as an opportunity costs to influence any busy time passengers to decide to choose to catch which kind of transportation tool which is the best right choice in the right time among of them. In the short time, for example, it seems any busy time passengers will choose to catch bus to substitute MTR underground train transportation tool, due to who feels the bus can arrive any destinations to compare other kinds of transportation tools in the most short time. However even if the MTR can either charge cheaper ticket fare to sell full day or charge discount ticket fare to sell in the busy (peak) time to compare to bus fare. It is possible that the busy time passengers will still choose to catch bus, if between the bus terminal and the another bus terminal that distance is the shorter time route to spend time to arrive destination to compare between the MTR terminal to the another MTR terminal arrival time . Also, although the busy time passengers will feel to enounter traffic jam to influence sitting or waiting bus time to be longer time in possible and who also feel MTR can avoid traffic jam problem. However, usually any busy (peak) time passengers will feel the chance of traffic jam occurrence will be less. So, the short bus route choice is more potential factor to influence the busy (peak) time passengers still to choose bus to catch.

However, if anyone wants to investigate results of day-to-day route choice which can be transferred to more realistic environment. It is necessary to explore individual behaviour in an interactive experimental set up to ensure busy (peak) time passenger transportation behavioural choice. For example, a passenger has a choice between a main road (M) and a side road (S) for travelling from (A) to (B). (M) is faster if (M) and (S) are chose by the same number of passengers. So, this method can be researched whether MTR terminal station is located at the main road (M) or the side road (S) where is more suitable to accept to passengers generally.

Why trip time reliability and crowding factors can influence MTR passenger choice? Other problem is MTR busy (peak) time's crowding in public transportation occurrence of MTR underground train transportation tool is becoming a growth to concern as MTR demand growth at a busy (peak) time. To capture the MTR passengers benefits with reduced crowding from improved MTR public transport service and image. It is necessary a identify the relevant dimensions of crowding that are meaningful measures of what crowding means to MTR passengers. Two main influences on MTR model choice that are growing in relevance are trip time reliability and crowding. It represents a benefit-cost framework. In fact, MTR passengers can be willing to pay more expensive ticket fare, it MTR can avoid crowding and short and the accurate arrival trip time between terminals is reliable to occur. How to measure of MTR crowding, e.g. weighting the gap between the busy time, the standard (i.e. objective) and the perceived (i.e. subjective) metrics. We are not in a position to definitely map the two dimensions, which is a crucial requirement for translating objective improvements into equivalent subjective gains that then can be applied, willingness to pay estimates MTR ticket fares to obtain the additional MTR passenger benefits of MTR public transportation investment to any terminal stations. Because MTR crowding has a negative impact on passengers in terms of psychological on emotional distress. MTR passengers are willing to stand for up to 20 minutes of the service is fast and reliable. However crowding outweighed these benefits from a MTR passenger's perpective, experienced crowding leads a increased dissatisfaction. e.g. stress and less privacy during who needs to stand up in MTR. Due to there are no enough places to supply to them to stand up in MTR. If the MTR trip time was longer time between the passenger's terminals, who will feel more dissatisfaction and it will cause who feels whether who ought need to choose to catch other transportation tools to substitute MTR next time. e.g. bus, train, tram, ferry, taxi etc. So, from an operator's perspective, the MTR service frequency or MTR size is significantly influenced by the level of ridership, which sends a signal to respond if the monitored crowding level exceeds the benchmark standard in the busy time. e.g. in the morning time or at the night time, the students or employment people who need to go to schools or offices (working places). The locations of different places between MTR terminals and crowding are regarded as a key service attribute for MTR pubic transportation along with other factors, such as travelling time and reliability, e.g. service quality, none engineering machines are broken to cause MTR stops suddenly.

Given the increasing importance of crowding on both the disutility to existing MTR public transportation users and the influence to it. MTR passenger can choose to use either the MTR public public transportation or other public transportation. It is timely to review the MTR current measures of crowding defined by transportation authorities. MTR operators ought evaluate whether they apporpriately reflect MTR each traveler experiences and perceptions of crowding in busy (peak) time. I suggest that MTR needs to buy other underground trains to supply to the busy (peak) time passengers to let them have enough seats to sit down, so who do not need to stand up in any MTR underground trains when they catch MTR underground trains in busy time. It aims to let who are willingness to pay the estimation of reasonable ticket fares to compare the other kinds of transportation tools in the busy (peak) time.

What is the crowding difference between train and MTR underground train? In fact, crowding won't be happened to brother these transportation tools easily in the busy time and non busy time both. e.g. bus, taxi, train, tram, ferry. Because passengers can not choose to stand up in these transportation tools easily, due to these transportation tools have no enough areas (spaces) to let them to stand up easily . So, the crowding will be avoided to occur in these tranportation tools usually. Otherwise, MTR will have many passengers who can choose to stand up because MTR design of length is very long and it has enough areas (places) to let passengers to choose to stand up, even there have none any seats are provided to let them to sit down. So, MTR passengers will feel more dissatisfaction and crowding easily, especial in any peak (busy) time every day.

Comparing to bus, much more diverse crowding measures are defined in the passenger rail industry. For passenger, different specifications for measuring crowding are found across countries and even within a country. For example, rail crowding measures in the UK, the passengers in excess of capacity is crowding measure that applies to all London and South east operators weekday train services at a London terminus during the morning peak from 0700 to 09: 59 , and those departing during the afternoon peak from 16:00 to 18:59 (office of rail regulation 2011 year).

The overall PIXC figure is considered the planned standard class capacity of each train service as well as the actual number of standard class passengers on the service at the critical point. i.e. the location on a trains of standard class passengers that surpass the planned capacity as the difference between the number of actual passengers and the capacity of the train divided by the number of passenger is within the capacity . So, it seems train and MTR underground public transportaton tools had been encountering the crowding problems in peak time, the difference in train passengers need to wait next train or more train arrival is who doesn't plan to enter the train, when who discovers the current train has no seats to provide to them to sit down in whose trip. Otherwise, MTR passengers can choose either to stand up within the large areas (places) if who discovered there are no any seats to provide to them to sit down or who can wait the next MTR arrival in order to who can sit down. It seems MTR transportation tool crowding environment includes in waiting platform and inside of the MTR underground train. Otherwise, train transportation tool crowding environment only includes the waiting platform and the passengers will not have crowding feeling inside of the train, due to none of passengers choose to stand up inside any trains because any train inside has no enough places to let them to stand up.

How MTR can attract many passengers. On the commuter departure time choice of any reference point researching hand, the departure time decisions of communters are of fundamental importance of peak period MTR traffic congestion. However, whether on the demand side, MTR underground train congestion relief measures, such as MTR ticket fare to every terminal station needs to be charged cheaper fare or discount fare in the peak (busy) time every day. To aim to attract many passengers to choose to catch MTR Underground train public transportation tools, substitute to choose other public transportation tools in the peak time.

Over the past decades, there have been very active research efforts in the departure time problem, both in econometric modeling and dynamic user equilibrium fields. Although, these works provide valuable insights into dynamic commuter decision making, they do not identify the commuters' response to gains and losses related to whole actual arrival time to reference points who may have relative. The appliability of the reference point hypothesis of prospect theory to the commuter's departure time decision making to obtain a better understanding of how departure time choice in MTR platform during their waiting underground train arrival time. However, every MTR underground train actual arrival time and deviation variables related to reference points (gains and losses) are the key factors in the departure time choice model. How the MTR underground train of every communter's daily departure time decision can be modelled when the reference point hypothesis of prospect theory. The MTR underground train's schedule delay is defined as the difference between the preferred arrival time (PAT) and the actual arrival time (AT) for a given MTR communter. In a daily MTR commute, a commuter in the indifference band actual arrival time is an essential feature of MTR schedule study. Two reference points are the earliest acceptable arrival time and the work starting time for a given MTR platform waiting passengers. In psychological view point, prospect theory proposes that the displeasure of a loss is perceived or greater than the pleasure of a gain of the same attitude and therefore, the value function is stronger for losses than gains.

To conclude, it seems that if MTR waiting passengers need not spend long time to wait underground train arrival in platform and it can provide seats to let them to sit down in the busy (peak) crowding time. It will make them to feel pleasure, even the MTR ticket fare is not fair and reasonable to charge higher fare to compare other kinds of public transportation tools fares. So the peak waiting time factor can influence the passengers to choose other kind of transportation tools to catch easily. Moreover, MTR's two reference points are the earliest role. Similarly a loss is observed when the MTR platform waiting commuter experiences or actual arrival time which is beyond that the MTR schedule time. Due to that a MTR waiting commuter is as an early side arrival of whose actual arrival time is earlier than whose preferred arrival time.

Reference

Bailey, L., Mokhtarian, P.L. Little, A. (2008). The broader Connection Between Public Transportation, Energy Conservation And Greenhouse Gas Reduction, Report Prepared As Part Of TCRP Project J-11/Tasks Transit Cooperative Research Program, Transportation Research Board Submitted To American Public Transportation Association in http://www.apta.com/research/into/online/land_use.cfmi, accessed 17 April 2008.

The UK Standing Advisory Committee On Trunk Road Assessment (SACTRA) (1999). Transport And The Economy (Report To UK DETR). Retrieved From: http://webarchive.nationalarchives.gov.uk/ 20050301192906 ; http://dft.gov.uk/stellent/groups/dft-econappr/documents/pdf/dft_econappr_pdf_022512.pdf

Wikipedia Contributors (2008). Arterial Roads In Wikipedia, The Free Encyclopeda, http://en.wikipedia.org/w/index.php?title=Arterial_road&oldid=212832640(accessed May30,2008).

What is the impact of transport on economic geography

Any countries must need road, sea and air transport to assist businessmen to transport products in local or overseas. If the country's road , sea or air transport system service quality is poor. It will influence any products transport time, speed, inefficient transport to anywhere. How to raise the country's transport system in order to improve efficiencies to let any businessmen can deliver their products to anywhere easily,e.g. warehouses, client homes, supermarkets destination in the most short time to avoid delay occurrence to let clients feel unsatisfactory or complaint their perform their delivery services poorly. I shall discuss the factors how to improve any countrues' transport systems to achieve the most efficient way as below:

Any countries' transport systems will create economic value, e.g. demonstrate value for money, economic worth, viable commercial worth, financial affordable worth, achieveable worth. Any countries' transport systems can bring welfare value by economics. It has direct relationship to take the form of measured economic activity, i.e. GDP. The form of measured economic activity can impact on any countries' economic economic geography, locally , regionally and nationally's local GDP impacts. The welfare impacts may include: leisure time savings, e.g. the local people drive cars or catch any public transportation tools to go to any geogrpahical location's shopping centers, big gardens, swimming pools, cinemas etc. places to carry on any kinds of leisure activities.

Environmental impacts may include avoiding noise, air pollution on road transportation aspect , when the main road is only on on focus on the main city,
but the city lacks other roads to let any drivers can choose them to drive, instead of the main road in the city. Then, when many cars are driven on the busy transport
time, e.g. morning working time or night busy time between 6:00 and 9:00 AM, between 6:00 and 9:00 PM. When either many working people need to catch public transport or drive themselves cars to go to offices to work or they need to catch pubic transport tools or drive themselves cars to home. Then, the only one main road problem will need them to stay themselves cars on roads, due to traffic jam or traffic accidence occurrence problem causes when many cars are driven on the road in the busy transport time. It will influence they can not go to offices or homes easily daily, even in the busy transport time, their cars' gas need to be used much to cause air pollution and traffic noise is easily caused easily in the busy transport time on the road. When the city has only one main road for drivers in the busy transport time. So, poor road transport system can bring poor impact on economic welfare benefits arising from proved labour supply from commuting, time savings, including exchequer benefits. Consequently, the county's GDP will be fallen down, due to labour market effects which do not add to welfare value.

Whether can poor transport system impact indirectly on GDP or not on local, regional , or national economic geography impacts? Does transport lead to greater economic activity i.e. higher GDP? DO they lead to change in economic activity location? Does transport impact the existence of business location and new economic activity opportunities? The measurement on every country's transport how impacts on economic change, facilitating geographic division of labour and specialization. It can be analyzed on these general aspects:

Costs and speed of travel time (Economic value of travel time savings) . Travel time savings to users from improved transport is a key of economic value, but it has only less influence,journey time reliability is more important to business frieght as well as business travellers, network connectivity enhancements as well as business travellers, network connectivity enhancement can help people and goods travel more quickly (i.e. linked to jounrey time and journey time reliability, as well as opening new destinations and new journeys, comfort and quality service provision is relevant to public transport, e.g. detering jounreys at particular times or by certain modes (e.g. overcrowding), impact on productivity at work for commuters, safety and security , due to loss of output from workers, transport accidents occur easily. All of these issues will impact any countries' standard of living to local people (geography) , even GDP income.

Why does the direct and indirect effects of transportation have a positive impact on the economic growth and development of a country? Does it influence acccess to goods, services and

employment opportunities in any regions? Underdeveloped countries must need to consider how transport system influences their economic growth. For example, the costs of transportation and production are reduced through timely delivery and enhancing the economies of scale in the production process, when the road is often traffic joam, gas cost, time waste , air pollution cost, noise has many roads, but if one lorry drivers needs drive more than one day to day to deliver goods to another city's warehouse every day. It will bring psychological pressure in terrible, when they need long time to drive on the road. They can not sleep easily because road accident will occur easily when they need to spend long time to drive lorries on the road.

So, how to solve the long driving time on road transport problem will be one issue concerns human life welfare benefit aspect, instead of economic benefit aspect. The transport system welfare worth needs to include human life worth. It is a valuable insight into the causality (ot lack of causality) between transport and economic growth and will serve to compare to any countries' national level and local geographical location level both.

In special, underdeveloped countries' public transport time whether it is long or short factor, it will influence workers their going to offices to work time. If they often need spend long time to catch buses, due to traffic jam,then it will influence their efficiences to be reduced, productive number is influenced to reduce also, because traffic jam causes they often go to offices too lately.It can influence workers' bad emotion to work every day. So, traffic jam will bring negative relationship between low efficiency and bad emotion to the workers, because they need to spend long time to wait, public transportation tools and traffic jam also influence their working emotion. Consequently, service and working performance will be influenced to poor, because long time traffic jam problem causes their bad emotion to work. It is one critical factor in the path of more widely spread economic growth and urbanization for traffic jam problem to underdeveloped countries.

However, transport system can also influence developed

countries' economy. How does it influence on environmental impacts aspect from mature stage. Its business activities must raise, dramastic expansion during this period, such as underdeveloped country, US, UK. In order to acheive long term sustainable development , new demands are being placed on transport sector, such as underground mass transit rail transport , ferry, local air frieght transport, train , e.g. Japan, Fance, US high speed prior rail. Because their developed countries , business and entertainment activities needs increase, it influences high time efficient and rapid speed public transportation tools needs are also needed in societies. These new technological public transport tools invention will impact on climate, noise, human health, land use and damage to ozene layer, acidification aspects, instead of economic beneficial aspect. For long -term sustainable development to be achieved, the various activities within developed and underdeveloped societies must be adapted to what can be tolerated by humans and by the natural environment. Transport is an activity which affects humans and the natural environment for both the development of society as a whole as well as for the mobility for the individual. For Swedish underdeveloped country example, air pollution in Swedish urban areas has beed reduced, but in many places concentrations of certain substances deiving from transport activities are still at unacceptable levels and much more has to be done. Carbon dioxide emissions and noise are examples of environmental problems demanding further efforts. Measures to limit the exploitation of valuable natural and cultural environments to protect biological diviersity are also needed. So, if Swedish still hopes to develop its tourism industry to attract many travellers to choose to travel itself country. It needs to solve environmental problems from different modes of transport are of different dimensions, such as improving its air transport to avoid cause different problems and rail transport differs in turn from road transport.

The transport problem to Swedish may include poor technological communication information to its public and purchasers of transportation and communication services as to the environmental effects of different solutions is significant in creating the demand for environmentally sound public transport service concepts. It is therefore important that such lacking high technological communication and information system is presented in as completem accurate and clear way as a method for non-monetary comparison of the environmental public transport service system aspect.

In real, it's public tranport service system is needed to be improved and upgraded in order to let travellers feel Swedish's any rail, underground train, ferry, bus , taxi etc. different public transport travelling service can provide excellent performance to serve their travelling passengers, when they need to catch any kinds of public transport tools to go to travel. They can feel convenient and comfortable to attract them to visit Swedish to travel again. Then, its tourism industry GDP income will be raised, if Swedish government can innovate any new kinds of purchase ticket equipment to install in and public transport stations to let travelling passengers feel that they do not need to spend long time to queue to buy tickets to catch ferry, train, underground mass transit rail on stations conveniently. Because long time purchase ticket queue waiting will cause travellers feel its public service performance dissatisfaction and they will complain , even they won't choose to catch the kind of public transport, even the travellers won't choose to travel Swedish again, if they feel Swedish is one developed country, but it neglects to take care about travellers' catching public transport travelling service needs.

It is one poor or bad feeing to let travellers choose to Swedish again. Hence, Swedish needs to improve its public transport service performance in order to achieve to raise their comfortable and satisfactory catching public transport tools needs to let travellers to feel. They may include efficient land use for transportation tools, comprising issues concerning natural and cultural environment, natural resources, biological diversity and aesthetics, noise reducing, public transportation energy consumption and time consumption reducing, raising public transport service facilities performance functions and other issues concerning the model. For example, Swedish government can facilitate the public transport price conparison and journey time spending comparison information gathering enquiring machines public transportation selection method of public transportation services to let every travellers can evaluate different modes of public transport when they are staying in ferry, bus, train, underground mass transit rail, taxi stations.

A travelling family can seek its sustainable transport selection system for passenger transport tool. When they touch the enquiry machine, they can compare busm ferry, train, underground train, taxi price and journey spending time from their transportation stations to another destinations. Then, travelling passengers can compare these public transport tools ticket prices, journey spending time immediately when they touch the public transport enquiring machines in stations any time. Then, they can make the most righ choice to decide whether they ought catch which kind of public transport tool to arrive the another journey destination. It is one every attractive high technological enquiry method to help any travelling passegners to choose which kind of public transport tool, it can be the most cheap transport tool at the moment in any public transport stations. So , for developed countries innovative its public transport service performance will need future passengers' journey needs daily. Hence, they can not neglect how to improve public transport service needs to satisfy passengers to feel satisfaction, if Sweden government hopes its tourism industry can raise GDP income in long time.

CHAPTER III

How globalisation influences transport development

It has close relationship between globalization and global tranport development. How globalisation impacts on the environment via changes taking place in the transport sectors. In fact, it is not clear how the relative price changes that result from openness will affect the environental composition of economic activity. For example, some countries will produce more environmentally intensive goods, others will produce fewer. On the other hand, liberalisation will raise incomes, perhaps increasing the willingness to pay for environmental improvement. These potential income effects increased outweigh the negative scale effects with increased economic activities. When combined with the positive effects with technology transfer, the net effect on local pollutants could be positive . Hence, we need to find methods to solve the problem of raising transport economic activities and serious environmental pollution creating as the same time occurrence.

Globalisation helps to facilitate greater division of labor, and to exploit its comparative advantage more completely. In longer term, globalization also stimilates technology an dlabour transfers, and allows the dynamism that accompanies economic activities to stimulate the development of new transport technologies and short time transport processes that lead to global welfare improvement.

On shipping transport industry aspect, shipping will increase ocean pollution, when international shipping activities are increasing. Trade and shipping encourages energy use in shipping is coupled with the movement of waterborne commerce. The estimates depending on the transport goods number of at-sea or in port days much increase globally every day. The energy demand of international shipping fuel sale number and domestically assigned fuel sales number also increases for global fuel usage. Estimates of ocean going ships now consume about 2% to 3% and perhaps even as much as 4% of world fossil fuels.Hence, when global shipping energy fuel usage number increases, because global shipping trading activities number increases. It will bring the environmental pollution to ocean level increases.

On air transport industry aspect, their travellers' catching air plans travelling needs and businesses' goods transport air delivery service needs are increasing from the requirements for high quality , fast and reliable international transport. Moreover, the networks that airline companies operate have changed often to hub-and spoke networks, many new often low -cost companies have entered the air freight market, any long time air journey is needed, e.g. Australia airline expands its one new air journey flies to UK, it needs two days flying time. It means that every flight to UK from Australia , it needs to use more fuel to fly. Then , air pollution will increase also.

On road transport industry aspect, global road transport cost and transit times, traffic jam occurrence chances also increase because when the road building number is increasing globally. So, it will cause traffic jam and long journey time spending , even fuel usage spending number is also increased. Then, accident occurrence chance is raised. Hence, global business or entertainment transport activities number increasing , it will bring much negative impact on environmental pollution, traffic jams number increases, long journey spending time increases, fuel usage number increases. Although , frequent transport activities may bring GDP income.

On transport service industy aspect, but is also brings negative influence to standard of living. It means that when transport fuel demand increases, transport activities number increases, GDP income on relative any transport activities needs industy , e.g. logistic demand needs, when lorry drivers need to drive lorries to deliver goods from one warehouse to another warehouse or supermarket or office etc. different business places on the road driving activities increase. But, it also bring air pollution , traffic noise and traffic jam etc. transport problems to road and natural environment and raises worse standard of living , bad emotion to working people or learning emotion to students , due to frequent traffic jam causes , low efficiency and productivity to workers, even student individual learning time can be reduced if they need to spend long time to wait bus, ferry, rail, underground train to go to schools , due to frequent long time traffic jam occurs on the roads to influence they can not go to schools on time often when they are catching buses to go to schools absolutely in busy transport time.

Thus, although any countries need to consider how to design their transport system, e.g. how to e.g. how to choose the right locations to build roads to let many cars can be driven available easily when the morning and evening (office and school transport busy time, e.g. 6:00 to 9:00 AM morning, 6:00 to 9:00 PM in the evening transport time usually because these two transport periods are usually , there are many students and working people need to catch any public transportation or drive cars tools to go back homes. So, enough roads number and long and not narrow road area must be needed to design in order to let enough cars be driven on the roads in the transport busy times to the countries have many big cities or have high population , such as UK, US, China, India, Hong Kong. They have many people , but drivers and cars numbers both are increasing. So, efficient road design and road number are also needed to increase in order to let drivers can transport goods to deliver, students and working people can catch any public transport tools to arrive any destinations on reads in the short time rapidly in order to avoid to spend long time transportation time and late to arrive any destinations in possible occurrence. So, any sudden traffic jam is not hoped to be caused by easy traffic accidents occurrence any time.

Hence, global efficient road transport system is needed, when global transport activities are increased, because any road logistic transport activities are increasing, they will also influence the students and working people when they also need to catch any public transport tools or drive themselves cars to go to working places or schools on the roads at the same busy transport time between 6:00 to 9:00 AM morning busy transport time and between 6:00 to 9:00 PM evening busy transport time. Because these both times will be have many students, working people , they need either go to offices or schools or go to homes. Hence, if the country had many lorry drivers need to drive their lorries to deliver goods on the roads in the transport busy morning or evening time in the same driving time on the roads. It will increase the risk to cause frequent traffic jam or traffic accident occurrence easily in possible in the country. So, any countries' governments can not neglect how to design roads and choose anywhere are the roads suitable locations to be built as well as anywhere land useful number to build road location choices in order to solve geographical traffic jams occurrence chance.

Hence, globalization of transport activities may bring geographical GDP growth, but it also bring traffic jams and traffic accidents occurrences, hearing impairment due to traffic noise, air pollution, traffic crashed, bad working emotions to workers and bad learning emotions to students, due to spending long transport time when traffic jam or traffic accidence occurs more easily.

However, transportation is an important tool if a country's progress. Rapid economic growth and increasing level of urbanization enhances a person's living standard have, it leads to a greater travel demands. Hence, governments ought not neglect have to design its roads , measure every road's length or width whether it has how many cars need to drive in morning or evening transport busy time for students, working people and delivery goods drivers of public transportation tools or private transportation tools easy driving needs in order to avoid frequent traffic jams or traffic accidents occurrences in possible.

Moreover, any governments also need to solve these issues, if they hope to develop their transport system successfully. These issues include : What mode of transportation to cost-effective in meeting a region's transportation needs to the country? How should a state department of transportation prioritize its highway delivers to maximize economic growth? What is the trade-off between additional growth in urban area and the cost of expanding transportation systems to accommodate greater growth? What effect does the expansion of transportation systems have on the need to invest in other types of transport modes? For example , the transport expansion may include the construction of additional highway segments, rail lines, runways, or additional sea, air, rail or bus terminal capacity using traditional technology; highway may include the additional of lanes to an interstate highway system; the conversion of an existing two-lane road to a four lane limited access highway, replacement or widening of bridges, and the extension of an existing road. Airport examples, include runway lengthening, apron expansion, and additional terminal gates.

On the other hand, enhancement to new transport technologies may bring efficiency of the existing highway system, examples may include intelligent highway systems, congestion pricing, intermodal freight facilities, geographic positioning systems, and instrument landing systems to mention of a few major transport innovations. So, transport policy makers need to understand the effects of these new transport mode innovations on economic development or GDP growth on transport activities growth transportation services and a more efficient use of limited land supplying scarce resources , air quality ,and noise pollution, traffic jams, long spending transport time to students, working people, entertaining people, even deliver goods lorry drivers their every day essential driving activities or catching public transportation tools needs problems. For example, the concept of intelligent highway systems needs increase trend. In simply , vehicles are being linked to each other and to traffic control devices to improve the efficiency of the total highway system. Similar types of innovations in intelligent traffic management are increasing needs for air, sea, and rail systems. The question is that whether intelligent highway systems can attribute of highways on economic development, raising on productivity of reducing highway congestion or improving pavement condition.

In fact, many developed countries' transportation system is mature. The nation has gone beyond the frontier of building, the interstate highway system and connecting most cities (markets). Tweaking the system with additional lanes and the new intelligent highway systems are useful in China, US, UK, because they have many cities. SO, road efficient traffic congestion control is needed when many students, working people, delivery goods transport people need to drive cars or catch cars on every city's roads in the transport busy time between 6:00 to 9:00 AM morning transport busy time as well as between 6:00 to 9:00 PM evening transport busy time.

However, transportation investment must be needed, if the country hoped to have good economic productivity, efficient transport service can bring good effects on the flows goods and people on roads every day when they use the country's transport system. So, any countries need to collect data, they can not be lack of enough transport information in any time that links anywhere locations of any drivers to the locations of the transport system that provide them with services in any time, e.g. every day morning and evening transport busy time, radio can report the real transport time of any roads traffic jam or traffic accident message to let drivers to listen to know whether anywhere roads are occurring traffic accidents or traffic jams or when the road traffic accident or traffic jam is solved to let the drivers can know whether when the roads can be opened to drive again. So, real time road transport message information is needed to report by radio, in order to let any drivers to know whether they ought choose to drive themselves cars on the road when they need to choose anywhere road to drive to the destination if they can know when the road has traffic accident or traffic jam occurs. They won't drive their cars on the road in the moment immediately.

On conclusion, globalization can being frequent transport economic activities. So, road , air, sea, transport service users' transport service needs are also increased. Every country ought not neglect how to innovate their transport service in order to satisfy their transport needs to achieve economic growth, efficient and short transport time spending, productivities increase, reducing air pollution, traffic noise , raisins. standard of living on transport influence aspect to satisfy working people, students, entertaining people, delivery goods transport users' efficient road transport time behavioral spending aspect.

www.ingramcontent.com/pod-product-compliance
Lightning Source LLC
Chambersburg PA
CBHW022104150726
47990CB00003B/1241